Saint Lucia

In the mist of the sea there is a horned island
with deep green harbours where the Greek ships anchor...

It was a place of light with luminous valleys

under thunderous clouds. A Genoan wanderer
saying the beads of the Antilles named the place
for a blinded saint. Later, others would name her

for a wild wife. Her mountains tinkle with springs
among moss-bearded forests, and the screeching of birds
stitches its tapestry. The white egret makes rings

stalking its pools. African fishermen make boards
from trees as tall as their gods with their echoing
axes, and a volcano, stinking with sulphur,

has made it a healing place.

Saint Lucia
Portrait of an Island

Jenny Palmer

Introduction by John Robert Lee
Quotations from the works of Derek Walcott

CARIBBEAN

To my mother and father

First published 1998 by
MACMILLAN EDUCATION LTD
London and Basingstoke
Companies and representatives throughout the world

ISBN 0–333–72981–1

10 9 8 7 6 5 4 3 2 1
07 06 05 04 03 02 01 00 99 98

This book is printed on paper suitable for recycling and
made from fully managed and sustained forest sources.

Design by Helen Ewing

Printed in Hong Kong

Preceding page: The Great House,
Cap Estate

A catalogue record for this book is available from the
British Library.

Contents

Fired, the sea grapes slowly yield
Bronze plates to the metallic heat.

Saint Lucia

Saint Lucia is a volcanic island 27 miles (43 km) long and 14 miles (23 km) wide in the eastern Caribbean, part of the Windward Islands and Lesser Antilles. Its immediate neighbours are Saint Vincent to the south and Martinique to the north. The population is about 142,000 in an area of 238 square miles (616 sq. km). The latitude is 14 N giving it an idyllic climate. The hottest season is May – October and coolest December – March. It is dry from January – April and the rainy season is May – August. Planes fly direct to the International Hewanorra Airport from many parts of the world. Inter-island planes land at Vigie Airport near the capital, Castries.

The landscape is very dramatic and varied, dominated by the famous Pitons, with rainforest, banana groves, hot sulphur springs and of course palm-fringed beaches surrounded by crystalline sea. The English have known it since Elizabethan times and the island is so beautiful that the French and English fought over it for years, ultimately to no avail as it now belongs to neither. Saint Lucia became an independent member of the Commonwealth in 1979. The legacy of successive occupation appears in the widely spoken patois which is a mixture of African, English and French. The languages now spoken are English and patois, but the place names are French, the main religion is Catholic and cars drive on the left – a delicious mix.

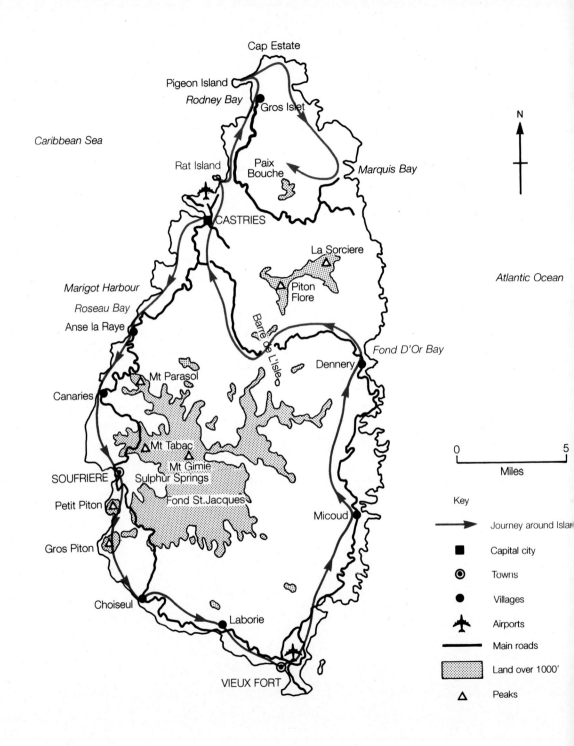

Cap Estate

Pigeon Island

Rodney Bay

Gros Islet

Caribbean Sea

Paix
Bouche

Rat Island

Marquis Bay

N

CASTRIES

La Sorciere

Atlantic Ocean

Marigot Harbour

Roseau Bay

Piton
Flore

Anse la Raye

Barre de L'Isle

Fond D'Or Bay

Dennery

Mt Parasol

Canaries

Mt Tabac

Mt Gimie

Sulphur Springs

SOUFRIERE

Fond St.Jacques

Micoud

Petit Piton

Gros Piton

Choiseul

Laborie

VIEUX FORT

0   5

Miles

Key

→   Journey around Island

■   Capital city

◉   Towns

●   Villages

✈   Airports

—   Main roads

▨   Land over 1000'

△   Peaks

Preface

Before I even got on the plane to Saint Lucia to create this series of pictures I called the most famous Saint Lucian – Derek Walcott. I'd read his poems at the time he won the Nobel Prize for literature in 1992. I was living in Cambridge and pining for the Caribbean to which I escaped every three months. His words encapsulated the deep feelings that particular archipelago engenders. In *Omeros* and his collected poems you can find many direct references to the island. I tried to find him at Boston University where he is Professor of English, they passed me on to the Playwrights theatre. Eventually, I tracked the man down in New York. He gave me three names to contact on my arrival: Rhona Pilgrim of the Sunshine Bookshop; Dunstan St Omer the muralist and Llewellyn Xavier the fantastic artist. This information formed the bare bones and the heart of my adventure which led to the following portrait of an island.

What a rich island at all levels. The visual level for me of course comes first – the colours and contrasts. Blues and greens dominate the Caribbean. The blues are shades of azure, cerulean, ultramarine and turquoise in the sea and sky, the greens are in the lush rainforest and on the leaves of bread-fruit, banana, plantain, aloe vera, calabash, cocoa, cashew, coconut and the seagrape. Then you have every shade of yellow and gold from the sun. Starting silvery at the beginning of the day it metamorphoses through egg yolk, golden and fiery to the bronzy oranges, reds and pinks of those incredible sunsets which have infinite variation and appearance. Finally, you have every other colour sprinkled at random in the exotic flower species – bougainvillea, porcelain rose, hibiscus, orchid, heliconia and the flamboyant; on painted houses and clothes – on people or pegged on washing lines.

The contrasts in the landscape are breathtaking, from the Pitons to the stretches of flat banana plantations. From the cool rainforest and waterfalls to the raw craggy boiling sulphur springs. Passing through Canaries en route to Soufrière you anticipate the appearance of the Gros and Petit Pitons but nothing prepares you for their theatrical presence and the truly stunning view.

Rachel Collingwood

Jenny Palmer (born 1963) trained in Visual Art at UCW Aberystwyth specialising in painting, printmaking and photography. Since then she has travelled widely while fashion styling and now runs a media resources company with her business partner, Rachel Collingwood. She divides her time with her son Joshua between London and the Caribbean.

Saint Lucia is an island that sings with its diverse talent – poetry, literature, painting, printmaking, carving, pottery, sculpture, calypso, soca, reggae and the jump-up.

There are many hidden surprises and magical places. Balenbouche Estate, near Laborie, is just one example. It is owned by Uta Lawaetz who in her huge historical plantation house, filled with art and antiques, has created a very special atmosphere. There is a display of Arawak and Carib Indian artefacts found in the grounds and ancient Saint Lucian maps. Horses graze beneath beautiful trees and you can walk down to the old sugar mill over-grown with the most graceful tree roots. Crabclaw plants, banyan and frangipani trees surround you. You can stay here in one of the specially individual rooms or simply take lunch or dinner while Uta tells you story upon story of the unusual history and previous occupants of the place.

Sir Arthur Lewis is the island's other Nobel Laureate. On his grave the plaque reads: 'Economist born 23rd January 1915 died 15 June 1991. First vice-chancellor of the University of the West Indies; co-founder of the United Nations Development Programme; first President of the Caribbean Development Bank', and has his quotation: 'The fundamental cure for poverty is not money, but knowledge'. Hence the Community College on the Morne is named after him.

I hope the book serves as memento of an island you know and love well; a guide to those of you lucky enough to be on a visit; or an inducement to book a flight and spend some time here. The photographs are arranged as a tour around the island starting at the Cathedral and Derek Walcott Square in Castries. Then up to the Morne, down through Marigot, Anse la Raye and Canaries to Soufrière. Then on to Choiseul and Laborie, through Vieux Fort to Micoud and Dennery. Finally over the Barre de L'Isle up to Cap Estate, Marquis Bay and Monchy and ending with a view through a banana leaf at Monier.

JENNY PALMER, London, 1997

Introduction

From Silver Point, home and studio of artist Llewellyn Xavier at the northern tip of Saint Lucia, you can see Atlantic surf surging in to Cas-en-Bas, the slipping shift of shade across the mornes, and nodding masts of yachts moored in the marina at Rodney Bay. From the artist's front door, you can look down the spine of Point du Cap, decorated with stylish homes and golf courses, and turn your eyes from often turbulent Atlantic to soft Caribbean. Your gaze is drawn up to the huge hump of La Sorcière, to the high range of Monier and to the undulating line of hills that reaches over to Morne Fortune above Castries and dips down towards the Vigie Peninsula and its lighthouse. If you look carefully, on one of those beautiful clear early afternoons, you can even see the tip of Petit Piton down the west coast of Soufrière.

If you visit the island at Easter time, before the hurricane season begins in June, you will see mango trees already parading blossoms along the winding routes, crimson cat-tails streaming through the hedges, bougainvillea pouring over fences in every shade from lavender to magenta. As you drive around my 'blessed isle' the colours, the birds, the landscape, the sheer island beauty of it, which you began to glimpse from Silver Point, keeps drawing your eye and heart.

I myself first began to observe, and therefore properly to see, my native landscape through the poetry of our Nobel Laureate Derek Walcott. And I also learned to write, after Walcott, of what I actually saw around me. I learned from the master of Becune Point that the best metaphor was found in the most accurate description of our beach-bordered landscape. Many visitors who come to Walcott country with his poetry in their baggage find familiar territory awaiting them.

The original inhabitants of Saint Lucia were the Amerindians – Ciboney, Caribs and Arawaks – who left us a few names and the traditional crafts of canoe building, basketry and pottery. My own great grandmother was a Carib from neighbouring Dominica. In Saint Lucia you can find Carib faces in Choiseul and down the west coast. Llewellyn Xavier himself is descended from Caribs and comes from Choiseul. Look at his round features and beardless chin, and you are seeing the face of one of our ancestors. Local archaeological societies will show you artefacts and take you on digs.

Historians have proved that Columbus never came here. Charles Jesse, the late English historian-priest whose *Outlines of Saint Lucia's History* remains the only general text available, records that 'certain shipwrecked French seamen discovered the island, calling it Sainte Alousie.' The Englishman John Nicol arrived in 'Santa Luzia in the West Indies' in 1605, only to meet with 'dire adventures at the hands of the Indians.' The English and the French then fought over possession of the island for much of the 17th and 18th centuries, until the matter was finally settled by the English navy in 1803. The island's official name became Saint Lucia, but its Amerindian name, meaning 'where the iguana is found', is commemorated in the name of Hewanorra airport.

Under the European powers the island's history was the familiar one of colonisation, enslavement or extinction of the native population (who resisted fiercely), plantations of sugar and tobacco, importation of slaves from Africa, followed by emancipation and much later, in my lifetime, political independence. The French Revolution came to these shores, setting slaves free long before the British abolition of slavery in 1834; so also did famous Britons like Ralph Abercrombie, John Moore (of later Corunna fame), and Admiral Rodney (commemorated in Rodney Bay). Local historians confidently point to barely discernible ruins near my home in the north-central hills at Paix Bouche, Babonneau, where the Empress Josephine's family had estates, to make a case for her birth here in Saint Lucia. In the twentieth century, the introduction of adult suffrage, a vibrant trade union movement, independence in 1979 and the growth of political parties have led to a healthy parliamentary democracy within the British Commonwealth – a thoroughly modern island nation whose constitution acknowledges 'the supremacy of Almighty God'.

As intriguing and enchanting as the landscape is to a visitor, the new arrival will also be struck by the variety of place names, so many in French, in a country that was once a British colony. I myself think that my country is more Kweyol (Creole) than either the French of its place names or the English of its colonial governors and their still-standing military barracks. The slaves, who were brought from different regions of west and central Africa, created a new language to communicate with each other. Today most Saint Lucians speak patwa (patois), a syncretic blend of African, French and English elements. Every October, thousands of Saint Lucians gather to celebrate Jounen Kweyol (Creole Day), on which only patois is spoken and Creole food and music, along with our distinctive national dress, are the order of the day. Saint Lucia shares its Creole culture and its patois with nearby Martinique, Guadeloupe and Cayenne (French Guyana), Haiti, and further afield, the Seychelles and Mauritius. Linguists in these Creolophone countries are working on a standardised orthography for this newest of literary languages. Many French Caribbean writers now use patois in their work. Derek Walcott, too, loves this second of his native languages and has included it in plays and poems; but he disagrees fiercely with the attempts to render its orthography straightforwardly phonetic, thus cutting it adrift from its roots in standard French.

Patois was once a despised tongue, forbidden even by uneducated parents to their school-going young. Gradually, through the work of the Saint Lucia Folk Research Centre, audiences throughout the island have been made aware of the richness of our Creole heritage of stories, songs and dances. And now, for the very first time in Saint Lucian history, our new prime minister, Kenny Anthony, has begun to address the nation in patois as well as English. He intends to enact legislation that will allow the mother tongue of most Saint Lucians to be used for parliamentary debates. Are we witnessing here the birth of a new Caribbean civilisation?

Meanwhile Saint Lucia is a nation filled with creative people. Artists like Llewellyn Xavier and Dunstan St Omer are well known throughout the region and beyond. In Xavier's gallery at Pointe Seraphine, Saint Lucia Fine Art, you can see a wide range of paintings and artefacts, not only by Xavier himself. Near Derek Walcott Square, in the heart of Castries, you can step into the Roman Catholic Cathedral to admire St Omer's fine murals. I hope you have a chance to visit St Omer's other church murals in Monchy, Jacmel, and Fond St Jacques (Soufrière).

Sculptors like Joseph Eudovic are recognised as far away as Africa. Calypsonians like the Rastafarian Herb Black, Ashanti, Invader and Educator, alongside female couterparts like Cheryl and Colours, Mary G. and Lady Leen, are household names. Madame Sesenne Descartes, the unrivalled queen of folk, has been honoured by Walcott in his Nobel speech in Stockholm and in recent poems.

But it's not all folk. The annual jazz festival is held in May, and we too

John Robert Lee (born 1948) is a Saint Lucian whose poems and short stories have gained him international recognition. He writes regularly for the Saint Lucian Mirror and produces programmes for radio and television. As an actor in Caribbean Theatre he led and directed his own theatre workshop. Whilst Librarian-Tutor at the Sir Arthur Lewis Community College, he developed the college's Creative and Performing Arts Programme. He is currently Director of Government Information Services.

have met and heard Wynton Marsalis, George Bensen, Al Jarreau, Nancy Wilson and Santana. Local luminaries include Luther Francois, who has played with many of the world's greats as well as famous Caribbean artistes like David Rudder, Len 'Boogsie' Sharp, and the late Martiniquan pianist Marius Cultier.

In literature, Walcott is the master, not only of Saint Lucian writers but of the English-speaking Caribbean. Even while living abroad, he often visited his homeland with his theatre workshop, and gave personal encouragement to younger writers like myself, Kendel Hippolyte, Jane King Hippolyte and Mcdonald Dixon. The seventies saw a rise in popularity of the 'performance poets', many of whom work with musicians. George 'Fish' Alphonse is the leading local exponent, a poet who has developed one-man dramatic plays out of his poetry. Walcott's proposed Rat Island Foundation, with plans to bring international writers to our shores (many of whom already visit Walcott privately), should help our local and regional poets, playwrights and novelists to achieve work of world-class quality.

So, whatever the time of year you decide on for your visit, you are sure to find all of us Saint Lucians busily at work, reshaping our cultural heritage – grateful in equal measure to our statesmen and musicians, our fishermen and farmers, our village teachers and computer wizards, our reggae stars and Nobel Laureates. We're creating, out of influences old and new, local and world-beat, out of and beyond all that history, in this present moment, a unique Saint Lucia.

Jenny Palmer's photographs are accurate sketches that portray the Saint Lucia that I know. Seascape and landscape, the people, their villages, glimpses of their lives, are all here. From the mornes to the quiet coasts, she has found an island that is still shy and private in so many pleasant corners. These photographs can serve as passport, letter of introduction and a simple map. Welcome!

John R Lee

JOHN ROBERT LEE, Paix Bouche, Saint Lucia, 1997

The Cathedral, Castries

Couple opposite the Cathedral, Castries

Micoud Street, Castries

'Rain', from Derek Walcott Square, Castries

Derek Walcott Square, Castries

Above and opposite: The Market, Saturday morning, Castries

The 'Saint Lucia Bellyfull' stall opposite the Harbour, Castries

Government House, the Morne

View of Castries Harbour from the Morne

Caribelle Batik

Angela in the dyeing room, Caribelle Batik

The Inniskilling Monument, Morne Fortune

Sir Arthur Lewis Memorial, near Community College on the Morne

Dunstan St Omer

House near Bouton on the way to Marigot

Joseph Eudovic

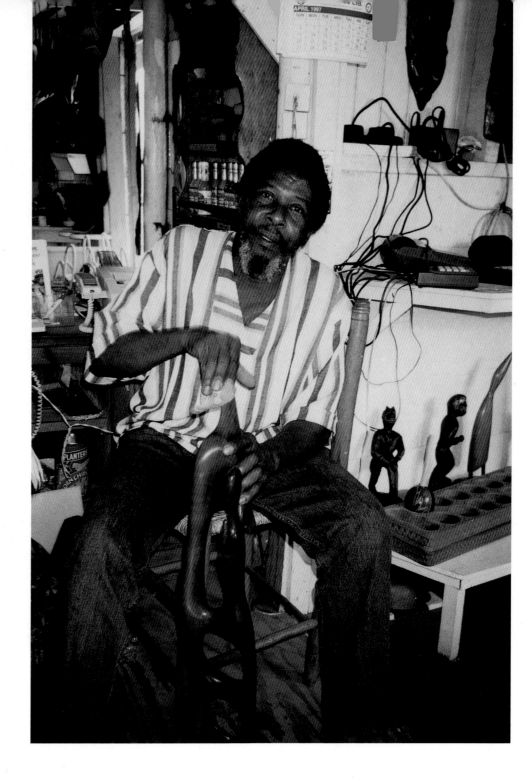

Opposite: Banana plantation

Marigot

Marigot Bay

Roseau Bay

Beach and boat, Anse la Raye

Fisherman mending nets, with mother and baby, Anse la Raye

Dunstan St Omer's mural of the Pitons, Anse la Raye

Anse la Raye

Portrait, Anse la Raye

Herb Black across the road from his yard, Anse la Raye

At Canaries,
the sea's steel razor
shines.

The Pitons

Opposite: Canaries

The beach, Anse Chastenet

Opposite: The Pitons and Soufrière

The beach, Soufrière

Church at Soufrière

Above and opposite: Soufrière

The Diamond Falls

Opposite: The Sulphur Springs

39

Crabclaw (*Heliconia Wagneria*), Joan Deveaux's Botanical Gardens, Soufrière

Porcelain rose / Ferrus torch

Morne Coubaril

A traditional bus, Morne Coubaril

Between the Pitons from Ladera, site of the Hilton Hotel
and Lord Glenconner's restaurant, Bang

Uptight's carving, Ladera

45

On board the *Unicorn*

Opposite: Boys dive for dollars, Soufrière Harbour

... where boys balanced on logs or, riding old tyres,
shouted up past the hull to tourists on the rails

to throw down coins, as cameras caught their black cries,
then jackknife or swan-dive – their somersaulting tails
like fishes flipped backwards – as the coins grew in size

in the wobbling depth; then, when they surfaced, fights
for possession, their heads butting like porpoises ...

Nigel on the *Unicorn*

Opposite: Marigot Bay from the *Unicorn*

Breadfruit leaf shoot, Rabbi's carving, calabash

Laurence Deligny aka 'Uptight', with his son Rabbi

Fisherman, Choiseul

'Joseph the Taylor', Choiseul

Shaving bamboo at Choiseul Arts & Crafts

On the road from Saltibus to Parc Estate

Family near Saltibus

Shingle rasta house near Saltibus

Cow grazing under palms near Saltibus

Uta Lawaetz at her plantation house, Balenbouche Estate

Balenbouche Estate House

The verandah, Balenbouche

Tree by water wheel, Balenbouche

Sugar mill, Balenbouche

Approach to Laborie from Choiseul

Bianca, 'Sea' and Ephrim at Laborie beach boiling up fish

65

Philoctete smiles for the tourists, who try taking his soul with their cameras.

'Sea', the fisherman on Laborie beach

Fisherman with conch shell, Laborie

Opposite: Saint Vincent from Laborie beach

Football by the Maria Islands

Fond D'Or Bay

Farmer, on the road from Micoud to Dennery

School children outside the Presbytery at Desruisseaux

Opposite: Sesenne Descartes, Saint Lucia's prized folk singer

My country heart, I am not home till Sesenne sings,
a voice with woodsmoke and ground-doves in it, that cracks
like clay on a road whose tints are the dry season's,
whose cuatros tighten my heartstrings.

There is a wide view of Dennery,
with its stone church and raw ochre cliffs at whose base
the African breakers end.

View of Dennery

Mending the boat, Dennery

At the wash house 'Over the Bridge', Dennery

Water skiing near Rat Island

Rat Island, late afternoon

Horses at the Rex St Lucian beach,
in front of Pigeon Island

Football and sails, the Rex St Lucian

84

On the beach, the Rex St Lucian

Howard Otway (right) on his boat *Reel Affair*, at Rodney Bay after a trip for marlin fishing and whale watching

Rodney Bay Marina at sunset

Gros Islet

Fishermen at Gros Islet in front of Pigeon Island

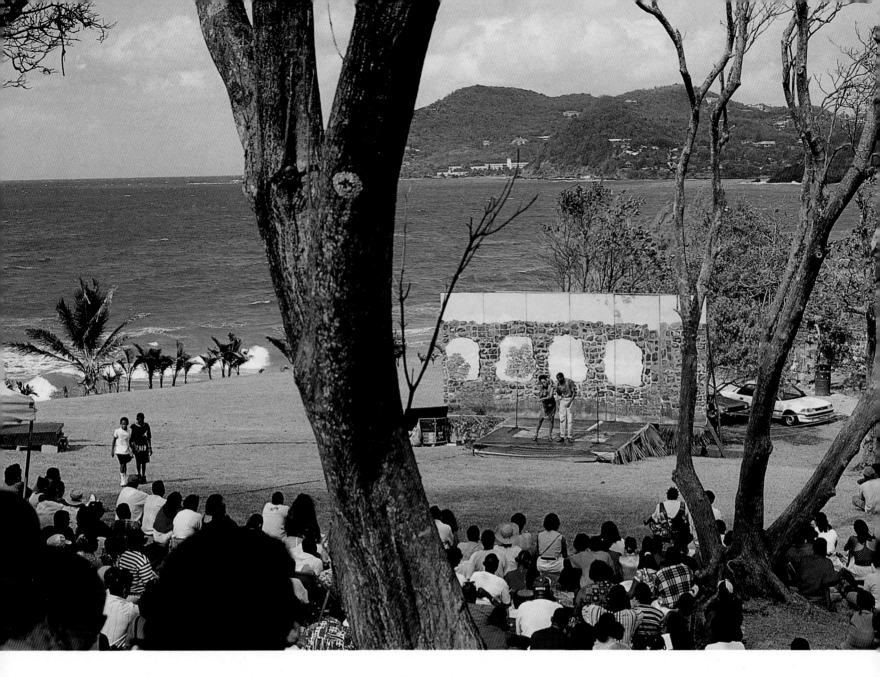

The Comedy Festival at Pigeon Island

The Pigeon Island Interpretation Centre

Boys at Pigeon Island

View of the causeway from Fort Rodney

Golf course at Cap Estate

Frangipani tree, Cap Estate

Derek Walcott, New York, September 1997

The seashore at Cap Estate

Detail of 'Caribbean Woman Dancing' by Llewellyn Xavier

Llewellyn Xavier at his gallery, Pointe Seraphine

Marquis Bay

Near Josephine's birthplace at Paix Bouche

Henry Alexander at his place near Monchy

View through a banana leaf from Monier

*... the claws of surf that made the sound
of a cat hissing ...*

When he left the beach the sea was still going on.

The seashore at Anse Chastenet

Acknowledgements

Derek Walcott, Rhona Pilgrim, Dunstan St Omer, Llewellyn and Christina Xavier, John Robert Lee, Sesenne Descartes, Howard Otway, Jane and Barbara Tipson, Maria Grech, Fenna Williams at the Tourist Board, Anita James and Adam Toussaint at Forestry, Chloe Wurr, Joseph Eudovic, Laurence Deligny and Rabbi, Richard Lubin at the Islander Hotel, Claudie at the Wyndham, Pearl and Ros at Caribjet, Frank at Transatlantic Wings, Continental Airlines, Nikon, Kodak, Dan Floissac, Uta Lawaetz, Henry Alexander, Alison at Caribelle, Herb Black, Francis Phillip and Bernard Common at Anse la Raye, Hermina Francis, Nature Tour Guide, Golinda Mathuin at the Desruisseaux Presbytery, Paulivette Fontenelle at Over the Bridge, Dennery, Bianca Collymore for persuading 'Sea' to have his picture taken in that beautiful light, Chris Perrins Edward, Ephrim Etienne *et al.* in Laborie.

The author and publishers wish to thank the following for permission to use copyright material:
Faber and Faber for extracts from Derek Walcott, 'The Homecoming' from *The Bounty* (1997), p75; Derek Walcott, 'Crusoe's Island', pvi, and 'The Divided Child', p30, from *Collected Poems 1948–84* (1992); and Derek Walcott, *Omeros* (1990) ppi, 47, 67, 76, 104, and 105.
Every effort has been made to trace the copyright holders but if any have been inadvertently overlooked the publishers will be pleased to make the necessary arrangement at the first opportunity.